Landmark
insights.
Book 3

Inventing New Futures

Landmark®

Landmark Insights. Book 3. Inventing New Futures

Published by
Landmark Worldwide
353 Sacramento St., Ste. 200
San Francisco, CA 94111

ISBN-13: 978-0692291573
ISBN-10: 0692291571

Printed in the United States of America
First Edition

This book points out what is possible if we step outside of what we know, and recognize and embrace our capacity to bring forth an entirely new possibility for living–not because it is better, but simply because that is what human beings can do.

Paradox and Possibility

If a cat jumps on a hot stove, he will never jump on a hot stove again. And that's good. But he will also never jump on a cold stove again—and that may not be so good. When something happens and we assign a particular meaning, that "reduces the likelihood of repeating things that didn't work as you hope it will, but that means you know less about the domains where you've done poorly than about the domains where you've done well."[1]

We are constantly engaged in scanning the universe for clues about what means what. It causes problems whenever our early experience with an alternative is, for whatever reason, not characteristic of what subsequent experience would be."[1] When contradictions appear, we are slow to let go of past assumptions to which our way of being and acting is correlated. Taking old assumptions for granted and interacting with things that are already settled limits us and leads to "just so much."

In recognizing that past, present, and future are an interpretation and not intrinsic to reality, a more fluid, open-ended, and relative world becomes available. We are never stuck with the way we are or how we see things. Transformation has the power to unseat us from business as usual, to upset the status quo—it carries with it a wisdom and a knowing that we have a choice about who we are and the full range available to us in being human. Ambiguity and paradox allow us to engage in a world that's nuanced, rich, and full of wonder.

Life Looks Different When We're Generating It

We were brought up, enculturated, taught, related to, from the idea that our subjective experience (thoughts, emotions, moods, feelings, etc.) has a causative relationship with our actions. That whole idea is really pervasive, tough to counter, hard to get beyond because it's so palpably clear to us subjectively. When we are excited (or bored, etc.), we don't say "I'm being excited, we say "I am excited." We take for granted that what we are feeling, thinking, etc. inside of us is what produces our actions—and that limits our world.

If we track down the false division between our actions and "what's out there," a whole other way of living becomes possible. "A dancer is locked into an environment, responsive to music, responsive to a partner. The idea that the dance is a state of us, inside of us, or something that happens in us is crazy. Our ability to dance depends on all sorts of things going on inside of us, but that we are dancing is fundamentally an attunement to the world around us."[2]

It's the way things "occur" for us that's the source of our way of being, our way of acting (not the other way around). Our world—a malleable, occurring world—is a function of our conversations, one in which we have access, where there's power, where life gets created and generated.

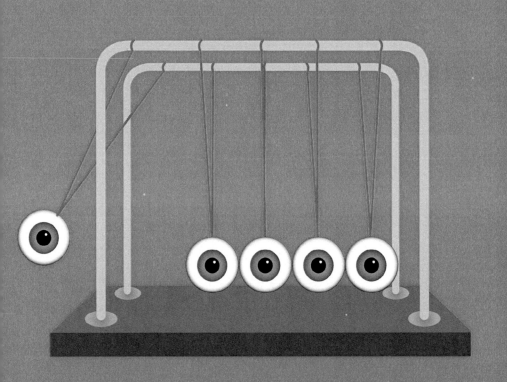

The Three-Part Myth of "Is, Because, and I"

Superman had issues with Kryptonite. For Achilles, it was his heel. For us, it's the three-part myth of "is, because, and I." With this myth in place, the freedom, power, and dimensionality available to us in being human are blocked–circumstances have the power, not us. How the three-part myth plays out:

- "Is" implies there's a "fixed" world out there–that things are just "the way they are" and that the only option available is to adjust.
- "Because" implies that the model of "cause and effect" is essentially a done deal–one thing causes another. Intervening or altering the course of events isn't logical or likely, and the only option is to adjust.
- "I" implies that who we consider ourselves to be is who we actually are, when in fact it's just a compilation of decisions unwittingly put together long ago to deal with failures to do or be something. Again, the only option is to adjust.

But the myth is in fact a myth. "Reality" is not fixed–it's a phenomenon that arises in language. Each moment's meaning "occurs" against a background of understanding, and how the world "occurs" to us lives in language–it's there that access to restoring our power lies. Reality is declarative, interpretive, and actionable–we have dominion in the world of *saying*. Recognizing that shifts our relationship to the world. It doesn't just lead to a different view, it gives us hands-on access to a world that's malleable and open to being invented. It's where transformation lives.

The Power of Listening

Communication, conversation, language are predominately thought of, anchored in our minds, as an expressing, a speaking, a vocalizing. That outward expression goes far beyond talking, far beyond describing or representing reality–it is in fact what allows for "who" and "how" we *are* in the world. It's what allows for the futures we create, where we evoke experience in others, where our ideas become clear and possible, where we share ourselves, and where others are expanded by our participation with them. But speaking is not where things get handled–it's not powerful enough. The possibility that there's an edge, the possibility of impact, lies in our listening.

Listening, we often think of as more passive–important, but somehow lesser or secondary. But listening is the clearing in which speaking can occur–without it, there isn't any speaking. Listening is an action. It's way more active than it is passive–it creates speaking. Listening doesn't receive speaking, it isn't a receptacle for speaking–it gives speaking. Listening is the possibility for meaning, for understanding. The possibility for being loved lives in one's listening; the possibility for learning lives in one's listening. Listening is what allows others to be–it's where both the speaker and what is spoken come alive, exist, and flourish.

Games Worth Playing and Openings for Action

In taking on big commitments, games worth playing, there will always be failures. Dealing with them effectively requires a special sort of environment, a way of being, in which what we have taken on creates an *opening for action*–like a "being toward" something.

When things *occur* for us as a failure, it's an interpretation, not a fact. (The idea that we can alter how circumstances *occur* for us is a central precept of transformation.) "The world is out there, but descriptions of the world are not. The world does not speak. Only we do."[3] When we know that, a *word shaping world* becomes a very real thing.

Possibility is not real at its origin–it's something we create as real, and then stand for as a reality. The conditions and circumstances will never be perfect. But in standing for a possibility, having the kind of courage that comes from a bold commitment to make what we set out to do happen, life is seen and related to differently–it becomes about redefining ourselves and reality at large.

When setbacks, missteps, and failures occur, instead of getting stuck in a downward spiral (which can sometimes be the worst kind of stuck), we course-correct, discover, and create magic along the way–improvisational flexibility becomes an essential art. Failures become a platform, a ladder, a means to fulfill the game we've taken on, and what it gives birth to, and what it attracts, what we can make happen, has the power to reshape the course of events.

GAME ON

"Yes"—It Extends Boundaries and Establishes New Playing Fields

"Yes" extends boundaries, establishes new playing fields, moves possibility from ideas to actuality. Actress and improv artist Tina Fey points to the opportunity yes affords us when she says, "the first rule of improv is *agree*–agree with whatever your partner has created. The second rule is *yes, and*–agree and then add something of your own. If I start a scene with 'I can't believe it's so hot in here,' and you just say, 'Yeah . . . ' we're kind of at a standstill. But if I say, 'I can't believe it's so hot in here,' and you say, 'Yes, it can't be good for the wax figures,' now we're getting somewhere."[4]

In our recurring dialogues, patterns of conversation, the habitual ways that we listen and speak, our first response often defaults around a "no" or a "but." Toss in a few intricately constructed reasons justifying that response, and we find ourselves limiting the future in front of us. For anything creative to show up in life–not accidental, not manipulated, not figured out–it shows up in our stand for possibility, in the "yes." Standing for possibility comes from *nothing* and creates a generative field; "yes and" extends that field and broadens the game. *Nothing* is the foundation for possibility–from nothing we are able to create with a freedom that's not available when we create from something. In creating possibility, we get to know what's available to us in being human.

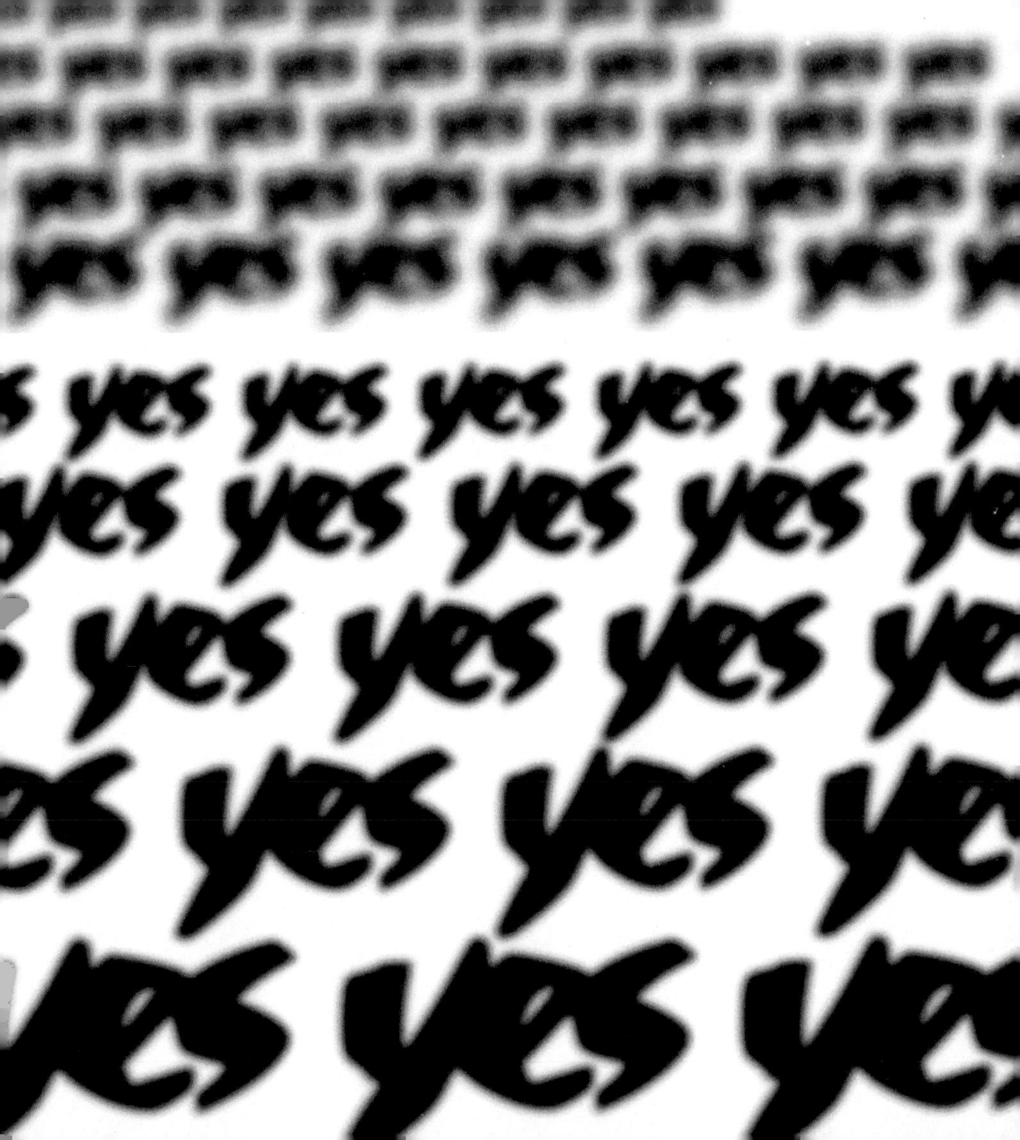

yes yes yes yes yes
yes yes yes yes
yes yes yes
yes yes
yes

Self-hood Is the Self Taking a Stand on Its Self

"...Our teacher asked for nominations for the best song. When I announced my choice, an embarrassing silence followed. I loved that song, but if nobody else liked it, I guess now I didn't, either. From that point on, when someone asked my thoughts, I'd have them respond first, and then express my opinion accordingly."[5] The pull for approval, for looking good, is a mighty one and embedded in the fabric of our day-to-day lives. There's obviously a certain validity and importance to looking good–the opening for action it provides, the doors it opens, etc. It's when looking good becomes the goal that it can erode our sense of self and limit experiencing any kind of mastery in living.

When maintaining any kind of pretense, we lose our self-hood and it's hard to be at ease. Yet it's not as if we woke up one morning and intentionally said, "Gee, I think I'm going to be inauthentic today." That way of being and acting is the already/always condition of being human. We didn't invent it, we didn't make it up, it's "just there." And it's against that gravitational force that we attempt to be authentic.

Self-hood is about the self taking a stand on its self–it's an existential act. Self-hood has no persistence–it doesn't exist in time, it must be created at all times, and that requires courage. When we are being true to ourselves, the already/always condition becomes stripped of its power–mastery in the art of living becomes possible.

ooo   gg poooxx

Our teacher asked for nominations for the best song. All hands were in the air.

a long and embarrassing silence followed. I loved that song, but

All hands were in the air.

ed that song,

but if nobody else liked it,

I guess now I didn't, either. From that point on, when someone asked

The pull for approval

embedded

is a mighty one and embedded in our language, our our shared

for looking good,

There's obviously a certain validity —the opening for action it provides, the doors

nportance to looking good—

the opening for

action it provides,the doors

it opens, etc. when looking good becomes the goal

ense of self and limit

experiencing any kind

of mastery in living it's hard to be at ease

When

maintaining any kind of pretense

e, I think

it's hard to be at ease

I'm going to be inauthentic

A Breakthrough Starts with a Creative Act

A breakthrough is something out of the ordinary, an extraordinary occurrence, an extraordinary outcome. Every day we are presented with opportunities to live as if it's "business as usual" or to create something beyond who we've been, beyond what we know. A breakthrough is not taking what's there and making it into something new or taking what is and changing it. A breakthrough is to take what isn't, and have it be.

To know what's possible tomorrow, we must be willing to *step beyond* what's possible today.

The Value of Money

The form and composition of money may change (e.g. livestock, beads, metal, paper, bitcoins, etc.)—but its significance remains. "Money is a fact of life, yet most of us understand it far less than we do those other 'facts of life.' And almost none of us has stood in its presence the way we might with a redwood, a Rembrandt, or a starry desert night."[6] It's worth looking at how we arrived at our ideas and values about money—how we were raised, the money memories we have, the array of inherited conversations, what money signifies about us, etc. (not to mention the seemingly random fluctuation of markets, fads, and industries). It's difficult to have an effective working relationship with anything or anyone when we don't know what or who is operative—or worse, when we identify something as something it is not.

When we get underneath our values to see where they came from, what's there is nothing—and from there we can begin to invent and establish values. In other words, we can go and create something we know that "we" created, and not be stuck with it, because we can again create something else. Sometimes it's not so easy to live with the contradictions between our old views and new perspectives, new values, new horizons of living. It's not a matter of tossing out our knowledge and experience—it's a matter of getting possible blind spots out of the way so there isn't anything between us and what we're engaging with.

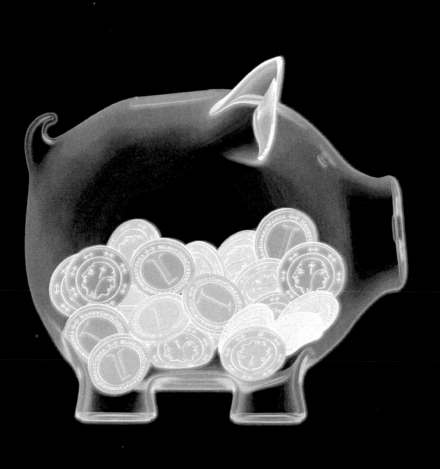

A Continual Choosing

Trails are made by the act of walking. Once made, we travel along the grooves that our own repeated action has made for us; the paths we take are well-worn because we take them every day, and we take them in part because, being so well-worn, they are the paths of least resistance and because venturing off the beaten path demands more work, and even risk.[7]

We can't help being aware of the *pull* (the attachment, really) to what we've done repeatedly. Even when we know it's not working, we often find ourselves reverting to old, automatic patterns, whether it's holding on to our positions, playing it safe, being right...Patterns established long ago many times aren't consistent with who we are and what we're up to today. Transformation doesn't merely change our outlook and actions, it uncovers the structures of being and interpretation on which we are grounded. It removes arbitrary ideas and views that limit and shape what's possible.

It takes practice, courage, and real work to give up old, unproductive *ways of being.* Choosing higher ground, inventing and sustaining frameworks that pull for possibility, forwarding the action, becomes a lifelong practice—a continual choosing. The more we practice giving up what doesn't work, the more the speed and frequency with which we free ourselves increase dramatically. An early-warning system gets built; new environments and courses of action get established. The outcomes extend in all directions and create the future like a possibility.

A CONTINUAL
CHOOSING

A Relationship Is a Grand Conversation

We sometimes think that the circumstances in our relationships keep our relationships from being great. (If only she..., if only he..., etc.) But it's not the content, it's the way we hold the content and the stand we take for workability that determine the quality and power of our relationships.

Power, fulfillment, and satisfaction happen if we take our various complaints, or things that we think don't work, and promise to produce what's missing—not as an insufficiency, but a possibility for something. Promising to produce what's missing leaves us at risk. If it's not risky, if it's a sure thing, if it's predictable, then what we'll be left with is something trivial. Courage is required to set aside our judgments, characterizations, and opinions and create our relationship being powerful again.

Being related is a grand conversation—it's living in a possibility, and if it's a possibility, it's inherently risky. And it's in risking ourselves, in revealing ourselves to one another and to those closest to us, that we become ourselves.

Reshaping the Course of Events

We take for granted that things *are* a particular way—and that it's the facts, realities, and circumstances that determine what's possible. We often, however, don't see the contexts from which we come that are shaping our reality—we see only what they allow. It is possible to have the same circumstances but to create and invent the *contexts for the content* with which we are engaged. When contexts are created or invented, it puts us at another level of effectiveness, freedom, and power—old frames stop defining what's possible.

History is strewn with times when major advances happened as a result of new contexts being created. Democracy, equality, relativity, human rights—new ways of understanding the world—were, at some point, *newly distinguished contexts*. In each case, some person or a group of people saw through or past "the way things were," or the way they "seemed to have to be." The act of doing so, and saying so, reshaped the course of events.

And so it is with being human. Seeing past our old assumptions and creating a context of our own choosing alters the very nature of what's possible—and the truth of "our" world gets transformed. Transformation has the power to upset the status quo, to unseat us from business as usual. To choose living a transformed life requires us to wrestle with our resistances, small and large, to come face to face with giving up our self-imposed limits and live consistent with what we know is possible.

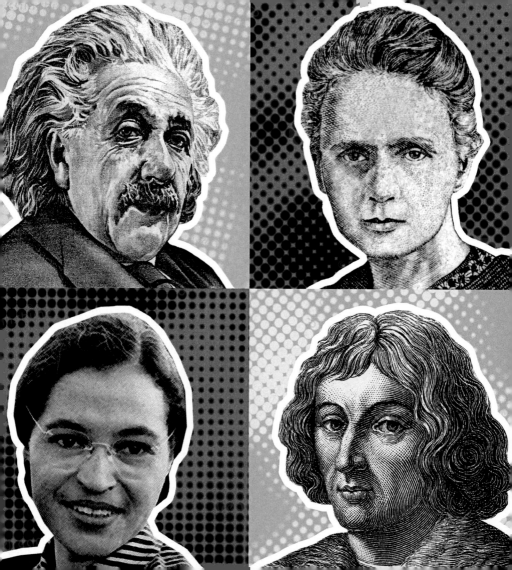

Values—A Platform for Our Vision, Goals, and the Difference We Are Out to Make

"...Almost anybody can learn to think or believe or know, but not a single human being can be taught to be. Why? Because whenever you think or you believe or you know, you are being a lot of other people; but the moment you are being, you're nobody but yourself." —e.e. cummings

In being nobody but ourselves, our values are always at play. Values are ongoing, they're never completed. They create a context, an environment, a dynamic equilibrium; they contribute a certain order; they service our purposes (the direction we've chosen for our lives, what we're out to create, the difference we are out to make). Values aren't conditions for satisfaction—rather, they are conditions for wholeness, for integrity, for fulfillment. They don't determine success and failure, but have a lot to do with our experience of being alive. We are never stuck with inherited values or yesterday's values; values are declared, made up, invented, created. We can invent new ones tomorrow or we can make the ones we already have "forever" values, but only because we *said* so—as it's in language that we shape, articulate, and define who we are.

In inventing an enterprise for our lives—one built on the foundation of our created values—our vision and goals begin to emerge and flourish, to invite a plan of action. They interact with each other, augment each other, accelerate each other, and become a platform for knowing ourselves powerfully, for making the unique difference we are out to make, for "...being nobody but ourselves."

A Place Where Magic Can Evidence Itself

The main presumption of existence is that life is one thing after another—that time is a one-way, no-return, take-your-lumps kind of deal. Hence the mild surprise with the question whether time has to go one way and not the other.[8] Our existence is a past, present, and future kind of existence, yet, past, present, and future aren't immutable facts. What would time be like, if the kind of time we talked about gave time? Suppose one could live not in time, but in possibility? If that were the case, a lot of questions that are important in time would fall by the wayside, and new questions would arise.

There's not a lot of excitement in a future given by the past. The only place the future exists (that isn't based on the past) is in our speaking and listening—we can create the future as a possibility by being a certain conversation. It's not a matter going to work on the possibility we created from our history out to a particular goal, it's a matter of working from that commitment back to the present. The commitment isn't like a matter of resoluteness, but something that wakes us up in the morning that literally gives us our life—it's a place that invites action, invites self-expression.

There is an enormous freedom and joy in living a life in the context of possibility. Living in time (past, preset, future) is appropriate to an "in order to," to "getting to" some place—to becoming; living in possibility is appropriate to *being*. It's not that it's magical, but it is magic—a place where magic can evidence itself.

A place
where
magic can
evidence
itself

A fundamental principle of Landmark's work is that people and the communities and organizations with which they are engaged have the possibility of not only success, but also fulfillment and greatness. It is to this possibility that Landmark and its work are committed.

www.landmarkworldwide.com

Endnotes

1. Adapted from James G. March, interviewed by Diane Coutu, *Ideas As Art,* Harvard Business Review (October 2006).

2. Alva Noë, *Life Is the Way the Animal Is in the World,* Edge: The Third Culture (12 November 2008).

3. Richard Rorty, *Contingency, Irony and Solidarity,* (Cambridge University Press, 1989).

4. Adapted from Tina Fey, *Bossypants,* (Back Bay Books, 2012).

5. Adapted from David Sedaris, *Children Playing Before a Statue of Hercules,* (Simon & Schuster, 2005).

6. Joe Dominguez and Vicki Robin, *Contemplating Money,* New Dimensions Journal (1990).

7. Adapted from Alva Noë, *Out of Our Heads,* (Hill and Wang, 2010).

8. Charles Petit, *Time Trajectories (review of "The Arrow of Time," by Peter Coveney and Roger Highfield),* San Francisco Chronicle (30 June 1991).

23289892R00022

Made in the USA
San Bernardino, CA
12 August 2015